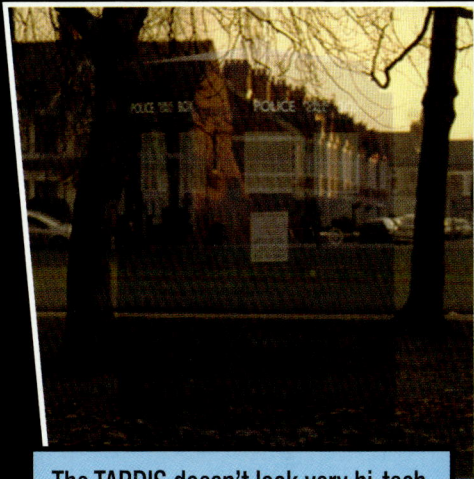

The TARDIS doesn't look very hi-tech, but it's capable of travelling through time and space.

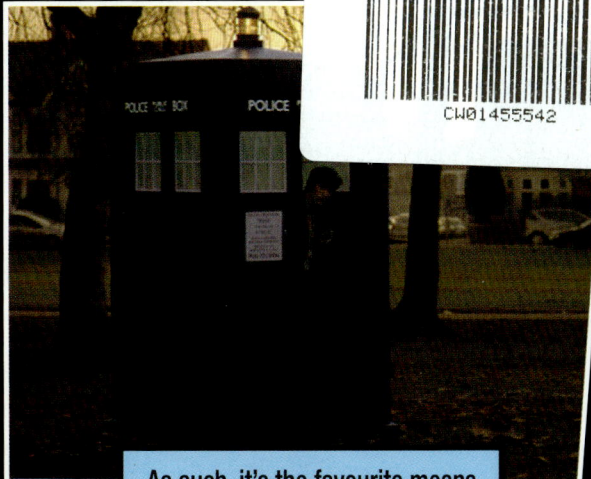

As such, it's the favourite means of travel of the Doctor and his companion, Amy Pond.

And although it usually works smoothly …

BZZZZZZZZ-KUN-CRACK!

DOCTOR, WHAT'S HAPPENING! IT'S SAYING WE'RE ON EARTH! ESSEX, COLCHESTER.

Unknown to Amy, the Doctor has been thrown clear.

The Lodger

Written by Peter Gutiérrez
Based on the television script "The Lodger"
by Gareth Roberts

DOCTOR, ARE YOU LISTENING? WAIT, DOCTOR, WHERE —

Chapter 1: Stranded!

- ARE YOU?

AMY!!

AMY ...

One day later. Nearby.

CAN'T AFFORD TO BE LATE FOR CLASS AGAIN. AFTER ALL, EDUCATION IS MY ONLY WAY OUT OF THIS ...

HELLO? HELLO, PLEASE? HELLO? I NEED YOUR HELP.

THERE'S BEEN AN ACCIDENT.

PLEASE, HELP ME.

HELP YOU? WHAT'S WRONG, SIR?

HELLO ...?

JUST. HELP ME. **PLEASE.**

LISTEN, I NEED TO BE SOMEWHERE –

I'LL LET YOU IN ...

PLEASE, WILL YOU HELP ME?

SOMETHING TERRIBLE HAS HAPPENED. PLEASE HELP ME.

With the lights flickering around him, the student climbs the stairs to help the older gentleman, who reminds him of his own grandfather.

In fact, he is so quick to help that he doesn't even notice that the door seems to close by itself behind him.

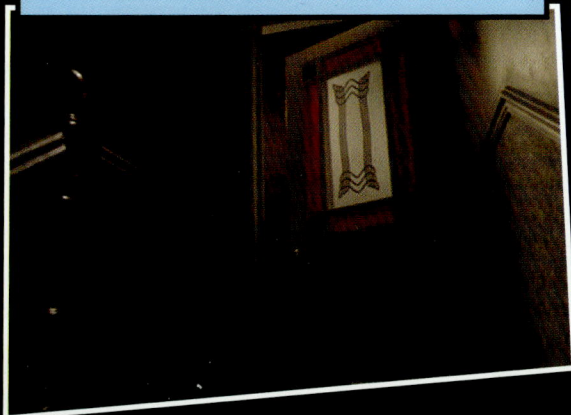

It's as if he had never left a trace of his coming ... or going. But he does leave a trace for those on the lower floor. It's a trace visible even to a casual visitor such as Sophie.

CRAIG, WHAT'S THAT ON THE CEILING?

Craig is paying so much attention to the tea he's making – and to Sophie generally – that he doesn't even notice when the mysterious stain ...

WHAT'S WHAT ON THE CEILING?

THAT! IT'S COMING FROM UPSTAIRS. WHO LIVES UP THERE AGAIN?

JUST SOME BLOKE.

... spreads.

3

SO WHAT'S THE PLAN TONIGHT? PIZZA AND TELLY?

SOUNDS GOOD!

BAH-BOOOMP!

FIRST THE STAIN, AND NOW THE NOISE ...

I DON'T KNOW. I'M TOO BUSY, REALLY, FINDING A NEW FLATMATE TO WORRY ABOUT HIM MUCH.

WHAT'S HE DOING UP THERE ANYWAY?

ZZZZ-uuuuuuuhhhh-kuh-crack

There is the faint sound of electricity buzzing somewhere in the house.

Their chat is interrupted by a call on Sophie's mobile phone.

YOU PUT THE ADVERTISEMENT UP YET?

YEAH, IT'S IN THE PAPER SHOP WINDOW. "ONE FURNISHED ROOM AVAILABLE IMMEDIATELY, SHARED KITCHEN, £400 PER MONTH."

WHAT? RIGHT. YEAH, BUT I'VE KIND OF GOT PLANS.

OH, ALL RIGHT. SURE. SEE YOU THEN.

NO, THAT'S ALL RIGHT. I SUPPOSE IT'S NOTHING REALLY IMPORTANT. IT'S JUST CRAIG.

SORRY, CRAIG. THAT'S MELINA. SOUNDS LIKE ANOTHER CRISIS AND, YOU KNOW, WE HAD SETTLED ON JUST —

Click

OH, THANKS, SOPH!

— JUST PIZZA AND TELLY, I KNOW. NO, YOU'RE RIGHT TO SPEND SOME TIME WITH HER.

REALLY? I COULD STAY.

SURE, IT'S FINE. I UNDERSTAND. SOME OTHER TIME.

WELL, THANKS. I REALLY APPRECIATE YOUR ... UNDERSTANDING.

Silence. They stare at each other awkwardly.

On her way out, Sophie can't resist stealing a glance towards the upstairs flat.

WAIT, WHAT'S THAT? MOVEMENT? AS IF HE'S STANDING THERE WATCHING ALL DAY ... WAITING.

MUST BE SOPHIE – LEFT HER KEYS BEHIND.

brrrrrriiiiiiiiiinnng!

I LOVE YOU!

WHAT AN IDIOT I AM. WHY DON'T I JUST COME OUT AND TELL HER? WHAT'S SO HARD ABOUT SAYING ...

BUT I ONLY JUST PUT THE ADVERT UP TODAY. AND I DIDN'T INCLUDE MY ADDRESS.

!!

WELL, AREN'T YOU LUCKY I CAME ALONG? MORE LUCKY THAN YOU KNOW.

WELL, THAT'S GOOD, SINCE I'M YOUR NEW LODGER. AND THANK YOU FOR THOSE KEYS. THIS IS GOING TO BE EASY!

HANG ON, MATE, I DON'T KNOW IF I WANT YOU STAYING. AND GIVE ME BACK THOSE KEYS.

YES, QUITE RIGHT. HAVE SOME RENT.

OH ...YES. IN THAT CASE ...

THAT'S PROBABLY QUITE A LOT. LOOKS LIKE A LOT. IS IT A LOT? I CAN NEVER TELL.

HAS ANYONE EVER TOLD YOU THAT YOU'RE A BIT WEIRD?

NAH, I CAN'T SEE THE POINT OF PARIS. I'M NOT MUCH OF A TRAVELLER.

THEY NEVER REALLY STOP. EVER BEEN TO PARIS, CRAIG?

I CAN TELL FROM YOUR SOFA.

MY SOFA?

YES, YOU'RE STARTING TO LOOK LIKE IT.

HA! THANKS, MATE, THAT'S LOVELY!

NO, I LIKE IT HERE. I'D MISS IT, I'D MISS ...

THOSE KEYS?

Craig does his best to change the subject in a way that he hopes isn't obvious.

BETTER BE CAREFUL. I'M THINKING ABOUT SOPHIE AGAIN, JUST LIKE WHEN HE ARRIVED.

HA HA! GOOD ONE, DOCTOR. SPEAKING OF KEYS, HERE ARE YOURS.

YEAH, YOU'RE WEIRD AND YOU CAN COOK – THAT'S GOOD ENOUGH FOR ME.

I CAN STAY THEN? THAT'S THE BEST NEWS I'VE HAD ALL DAY. I'LL MOVE MY STUFF IN AS SOON AS I BUY SOME STUFF THAT I CAN MOVE IN.

GREAT! MY KEYS. MY PLACE. MY ...

... ROT.

BY THE WAY, ABOUT THAT ROT ... I'VE GOT THE STRANGEST FEELING WE ...

... SHOULDN'T TOUCH IT.

That evening, the Doctor uses the communicator in his ear to contact Amy in the TARDIS.

EARTH TO POND, EARTH TO POND ...

COME IN, POND.

DOCTOR!!

COULD YOU NOT WRECK MY NEW EARPIECE, POND?

OOOOH. SORRY ABOUT THAT!

HOW'S THE TARDIS COPING?

SEE FOR YOURSELF. I MEAN, LISTEN FOR YOURSELF.

OOH, NASTY. SHE'S LOCKED IN A MATERIALISATION LOOP, TRYING TO LAND AGAIN.

NO SIGN OF THAT. MY READINGS SAY THAT WHATEVER'S STOPPING THE TARDIS IS UPSTAIRS IN THAT FLAT ...

THAT'S BAD. THAT COULD MEAN TIME ITSELF MIGHT START TO REPEAT.

I DON'T KNOW WHAT IT IS, THOUGH. ANYTHING THAT CAN STOP THE TARDIS FROM LANDING IS BIG.

SCARY BIG!

SO GO UPSTAIRS AND SORT IT!

ME? OF COURSE NOT. BESIDES, I'VE GOT CRAIG HERE TO HELP ME.

WAIT ... ARE YOU SCARED?

... I MEAN, HE'S A BIT WEIRD. BUT GOOD WEIRD, YOU KNOW?

... THE LODGER UPSTAIRS.

WOW, THAT WAS SOME PARTY. BUT IF I DON'T GET A MOVE-ON, I'LL MISS THE LAST TRAIN HOME.

HELLO. STOP, PLEASE. CAN YOU HEAR ME? I NEED YOUR HELP.

HMM, SOUNDS LIKE A NICE POLITE FELLOW. GUESS THERE'S NO HARM SEEING WHAT HE WANTS ...

PLEASE. MY LITTLE GIRL'S HURT.

OH, THAT'S A HARD ONE TO REFUSE.

I'M SO SORRY, BUT WILL YOU HELP ME? PLEASE.

HELP YOU?

Of course the poor woman doesn't know that actually *she's* the one who needs help.

MUMBLE-MUMBLE

ORANGE JUICE GRAVY, DAINTY RHINO, DANCING THEIR HUNGER AWAY.

HANG ON A SEC, SOPH.

WHAT IS IT, CRAIG? EVERYTHING ALL RIGHT?

IN OTHER WORDS, POND, I CAN'T GO UP THERE UNTIL I KNOW WHAT I'M DEALING WITH. IT'S VITAL THAT THIS 'MAN' UPSTAIRS DOESN'T REALISE WHO AND WHAT I AM!

... AND A HEDGEHOG HARNESS, TOO.

IN FACT, I CAN USE MY EARPIECE ONLY BECAUSE IT'S SET TO 'SCRAMBLE'. TO ANYONE ELSE, WE'RE TALKING ABSOLUTE GIBBERISH.

SOPHIE'S 'MAD SCIENTIST' MAY BE CORRECT AFTER ALL. I CAN'T WASTE MY TIME ON THIS NONSENSE.

HMM. HERE'S ONE ... BOW TIE – GET RID!

ALL I'VE GOT TO DO IS PASS AS AN ORDINARY HUMAN BEING. SIMPLE. ANY HELPFUL HINTS?

I THOUGHT BOW TIES WERE COOL. LIKE SUNGLASSES. COME ON, AMY, TELL ME WHAT NORMAL BLOKES DO.

CRAAAASSSSHH!

Suddenly the Doctor knows that the time has come to stop playing with sunglasses and talking about the telly.

THEY WATCH TELLY, THEY PLAY FOOTBALL ...

I COULD DO THOSE THINGS! I DON'T, BUT I COULD ...

HANG ON, THERE'S BEEN ANOTHER LOUD – AMY? ARE YOU THERE?

AMY?!

DOCTOR ...!!

Rrruuummble rumble-RUUUUUMBLE–

Time is supposed to move forward ... not sideways. It also shouldn't repeat itself. The Doctor, a master of time travel, tries not to become alarmed by what he sees.

INTERESTING. LOCALISED TIME LOOP.

AAAAAAHHHHHH!

TIME DISTORTION. AMY, WHATEVER'S HAPPENING UPSTAIRS, IS STILL AFFECTING YOU.

AMY, ARE YOU ALL RIGHT? I THOUGHT I HEARD YOU SCREAM ...

YES, I WAS SCREAMING, THANK YOU. BUT EVERYTHING ...

SEEMS ALL RIGHT AGAIN NOW.

IT'S ... STOPPED.

THANK GOODNESS!

ALL RIGHT, I'LL NEED TO ACT SOONER THAN I PLANNED ... **AND** LOOK NORMAL.

Chapter 3: The Man Upstairs

The next morning, Craig and the Doctor go about their business as if nothing had happened the night before.

LA LA LA! THE RAIN IN SPAIN ...

DOCTOR! HOW LONG ARE YOU GOING TO BE IN THERE?

OH, SORRY, I LIKE A GOOD SOAK!

KUH-BAMₚF!

DOCTOR, DID YOU HEAR THAT? WHAT WAS IT?

Soon after ...

YES? HELLO?

IT'S ME, CRAIG, FROM DOWNSTAIRS. I HEARD A LOUD BANG – ARE YOU ALL RIGHT?

WHAT DID YOU SAY?

WELL, I'LL JUST GO UPSTAIRS – SEE IF HE'S OKAY.

I ...

WAIT, CRAIG! DID YOU SAY 'UPSTAIRS'?

THANK YOU, CRAIG, BUT I DON'T NEED YOUR HELP.

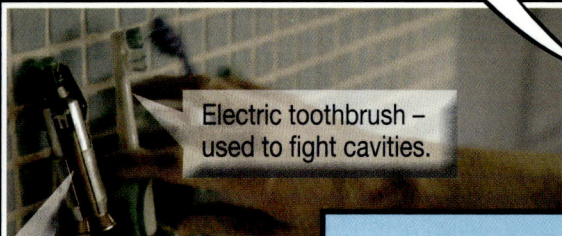

Electric toothbrush – used to fight cavities.

OH ... ALL RIGHT, THEN.

Sonic Screwdriver – used to open tricky locks – and a thousand other uses.

In his rush, and with a bit of soap in his eyes, the Doctor makes an understandable mistake.

HIS VOICE IS SO CALM AND PLEASANT BUT AT THE SAME TIME NOT QUITE ...

AH! HELLO! MY NAME'S THE DOCTOR!
OH, HELLO!
RIGHT. YOU MUST BE SOPHIE.
MM-HM.
PLEASURE. SEE YOU IN A BIT, THEN, I'M SURE.
Moments later …
YOU WILL? REALLY? THANKS, DOCTOR, YOU'VE SAVED MY LIFE! WITH DOM DOWN WITH A BUG, WE'D BE A PLAYER SHORT.
SURE, I'D LOVE TO BE ON YOUR FOOTBALL TEAM. AFTER ALL, BLOKES PLAY FOOTBALL, DON'T THEY? IN FACT, I'M VERY GOOD AT FOOTBALL …
I THINK.
OH, THIS SHOULD BE INTERESTING!
UH-OH – I'M NOT SURE I LIKE HER FINDING HIM SO 'INTERESTING'.
SO YOU'LL BE AT THE MATCH, TOO, SOPHIE?
I WOULDN'T MISS IT FOR THE WORLD!

The Doctor retreats to his room until a thought hits him.

SOPHIE, WAIT, HOW DID YOU UNLOCK THE FRONT DOOR? THOSE ARE YOUR KEYS OVER THERE. YOU MUST HAVE LEFT THEM LAST TIME YOU CAME HERE.

I – I'VE BEEN HOLDING THEM!

YEAH, BUT I ...

IT'S ALL RIGHT. I DO HAVE ANOTHER SET.

YOU'VE GOT TWO SETS OF KEYS TO SOMEONE ELSE'S HOUSE?

The Doctor soon updates Amy on his plans.

UM, YEAH.

I SEE! YOU MUST LIKE IT HERE, TOO.

SO I'M GOING OUT. IF I HANG ABOUT THE HOUSE ALL THE TIME, THE MAN UPSTAIRS MIGHT GET SUSPICIOUS.

FOOTBALL? OKAY, WELL DONE. THAT **IS** NORMAL. YOU SHOULD BE ABLE TO BLEND IN WELL.

FOOTBALL'S THE ONE WITH THE STICKS, ISN'T IT?

YEAH. I'LL LOVE IT, I THINK. ALL OUTDOORSY AND SO FORTH.

BUT A QUICK QUESTION ...

WHAT ARE YOU ACTUALLY CALLED – WHAT'S YOUR PROPER NAME?

JUST CALL ME 'THE DOCTOR'.

THAT'S FINE FOR ME, BUT I CAN'T JUST SAY TO THESE GUYS, "HEY, THIS IS MY NEW FLATMATE. HE'S CALLED THE DOCTOR."

WHY NOT?

BECAUSE

IT'S

WEIRD.

Soon they are greeted by one of Craig's team mates.

ALL RIGHT, UM, *DOCTOR*. I'M SEAN. WHERE ARE YOU STRONGEST?

ARMS.

NO, HE MEANS, WHAT POSITION ON THE FIELD.

LET'S FIND OUT!

NOT SURE. THE FRONT? THE SIDE?

... BELOW?

OH, A COMEDIAN. THAT'LL HELP TEAM MORALE. ARE YOU ANY GOOD, THOUGH?

The Doctor kicks the ball onto the pitch, and that's how it begins … a football match that few who saw it would ever forget …

The Doctor intercepts passes without hesitation.

And he's unstoppable whenever he drives with the ball.

Most importantly, he scores goals.

And then more goals.

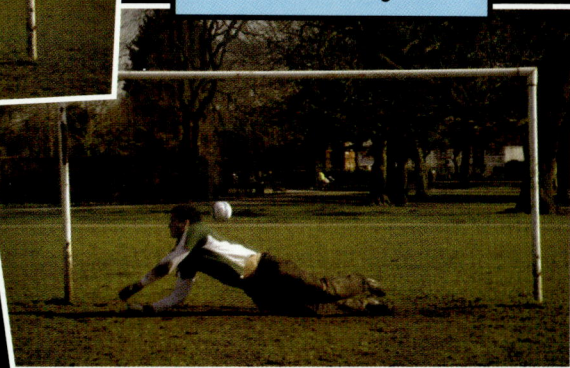

GO, DOCTOR! GO, DOCTOR!

Craig, of course, is not thrilled with how his new team mate seems to be outshining him in Sophie's eyes.

But Sophie isn't the only one cheering on the Doctor.

Soon the onlookers begin a chant that grows and grows.

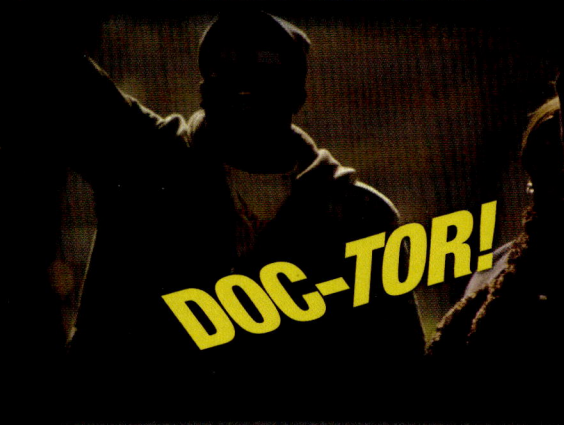

DOC-TOR!

DOC-TOR!

DOC-TOR!

In fact, the longer they play, the more the Doctor simply takes over the match.

In the end, it seems not so much that a team has been victorious, but a single man.

Meanwhile, on a familiar street.
SO MUCH TO DO! AND IF I DON'T MAKE IT TO THE PASSPORT OFFICE BEFORE IT CLOSES, I WON'T GET ANOTHER CHANCE UNTIL NEXT WEEK AND –
PLEASE CAN YOU HELP? CAN YOU ...
The woman who is in so much of a rush is surprised to find herself stopping. She wouldn't usually, but it's a **little girl's** voice that she hears.
A little girl who needs help. She sounds so **alone**, so **scared**.
... HELP?
HELLO?
I'VE LOST MY MUM. I DON'T KNOW WHERE SHE IS. PLEASE, CAN YOU HELP ME?
HELP YOU? YOU POOR THING. WHAT'S HAPPENED?
CAN YOU HELP ME FIND HER?
CERTAINLY, DON'T WORRY! I'LL BE GLAD TO COME UP AND ...
... HELP YOU.

Later, that evening ...

DOCTOR!

?!

HELLO.

THAT'S GOT BIGGER, HASN'T IT?

BUT SOPHIE, I WANT TO TELL YOU ...

I DON'T MIND THAT IT'S THERE. I'D STILL PREFER TO STAY IN WITH YOU.

WHAT ARE YOU DOING DOWN THERE? I THOUGHT YOU WERE GOING OUT.

HE REALLY IS ON HIS WAY OUT.

UM, I DON'T MIND, IF YOU DON'T MIND.

WHOOPS, SORRY. I WAS IN A WORLD OF MY OWN DOWN THERE, RE-CONNECTING ALL THE ELECTRICS. IT'S A REAL MESS.

I DON'T MIND – WHY WOULD I MIND?

DID I JUST MESS THINGS UP? WAS CRAIG GOING TO TEL ME SOMETHING?

And so instead of an evening during which Craig hoped to tell Sophie his true feelings for her, he ends up listening to her confide in the Doctor.

SO, THE CALL CENTRE IS NO GOOD THEN? WHAT DO YOU REALLY WANT TO DO?

LIFE CAN SEEM SO POINTLESS, DOCTOR. WORK, WEEKEND, WORK, WEEKEND.

DON'T LAUGH – I WANT TO WORK WITH ORANGUTANS.

WHAT'S STOPPING YOU?

IT'S SCARY TO THINK ABOUT MOVING ABROAD. EVERYONE I KNOW LIVES ROUND HERE. CRAIG GOT OFFERED A JOB IN LONDON, BETTER MONEY, BUT HE DIDN'T TAKE IT.

WELL, SOPHIE, YOU'LL JUST HAVE TO STAY HERE – SECURE AND A BIT MISERABLE UNTIL THE DAY YOU DROP. BETTER THAN TRYING AND FAILING, EH?

WHAT'S WRONG WITH STAYING HERE? I CAN'T SEE THE POINT OF MOVING TO LONDON.

YOU THINK I'D **FAIL**?

EVERYBODY'S GOT DREAMS, SOPHIE, BUT VERY FEW ACHIEVE THEM. PERHAPS, IN THE WHOLE UNIVERSE, A CALL CENTRE IS WHERE YOU SHOULD BE.

YES, BUT IS IT TRUE?

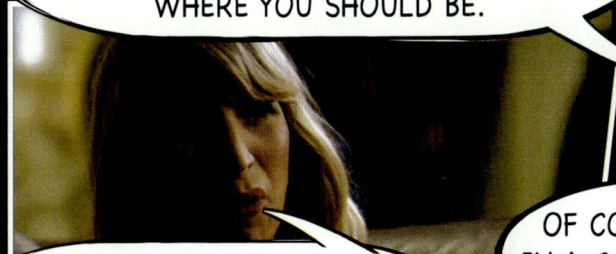

WHY ARE YOU SAYING THAT? THAT'S HORRIBLE.

OF COURSE NOT! I'M NOT STAYING IN A CALL CENTRE ALL MY LIFE! I CAN DO ANYTHING I WANT!

IT'S A BIG OLD WORLD, SOPHIE. WORK OUT WHAT'S REALLY KEEPING YOU HERE, EH?

SO, ARE YOU GOING TO BE TAKING OFF THEN? SEEING THE WORLD? SAVING MONKEYS?

When it's time to say goodnight, Craig tries to keep his tone light. After all, he's only a 'friend'.

WHAT? DO YOU THINK I SHOULD?

YEAH ... LIKE THE DOCTOR SAYS, WHAT'S KEEPING YOU HERE?

29

Some time later, the Doctor addresses the problem of what's keeping him there instead of rejoining Amy on the TARDIS.

A master of technology, the Doctor has built a scanner that can help him understand the enemy they face.

SHIELD'S UP. LET'S SCAN!

WHAT ARE YOU GETTING?

If it doesn't bash him in the head, that is.

IT SEEMS THERE ARE NO TRACES OF HIGH TECHNOLOGY UPSTAIRS. IT'S COMPLETELY NORMAL ...

LOOK, YOU SAID I COULD BE LOST FOREVER. JUST GO UPSTAIRS, PLEASE.

BUT WITHOUT KNOWING WHAT I'M UP AGAINST, I COULD GET MYSELF KILLED. THEN YOU'D **REALLY** BE LOST. IF I COULD JUST GET A LOOK IN THERE ...

AMY, USE THE DATA BANK, GET ME THE PLANS OF THIS BUILDING – ITS HISTORY, THE LAYOUT, **EVERYTHING**.

HOLD ON!

WILL DO.

THANKS. MEANWHILE, I SHALL RECRUIT ...

... A SPY.

As Craig tidies up, he realises that Sophie was right. The stain *was* getting bigger and bigger.

SO MUCH FOR MR 'I-CAN-FIX-ROT'. I'LL SHOW HIM THAT I CAN HANDLE PROBLEMS IN MY OWN FLAT, THANK YOU VERY MUCH.

SIZZZZLE

OW!

Craig passes out in his bedroom almost immediately, and it is in this state that the Doctor finds him when he delivers breakfast the next morning.

CRAIG, I TOLD YOU NOT TO TOUCH THAT STAIN! WAIT, WHAT'S THAT?

NICE GOING, CRAIG! HERE WE HAVE A POSSIBLY POISONOUS SUBSTANCE. "OH, I KNOW WHAT WOULD BE REALLY CLEVER. I'LL STICK MY HAND IN IT!"

COME ON, CRAIG, BREATHE! USE THOSE HEALTHY FOOTBALLER'S LUNGS!

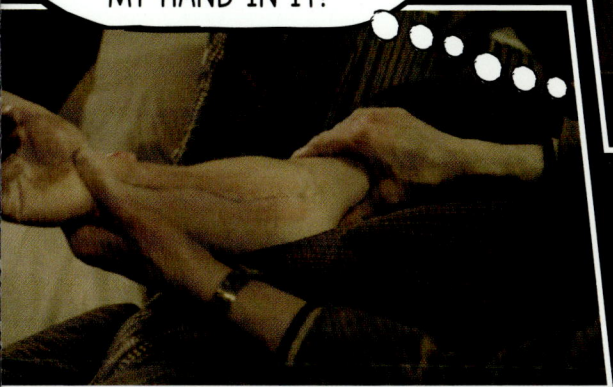

GASP!

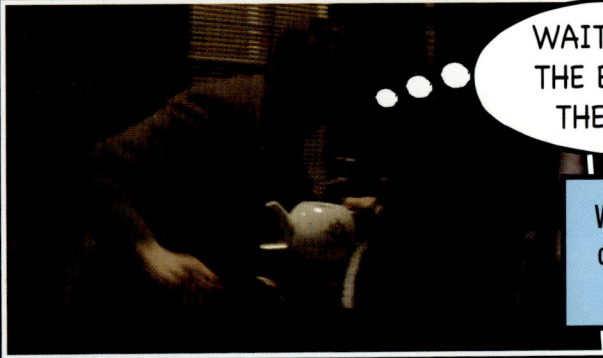

WAIT – I NEED TO REVERSE THE ENZYME DECAY. EXCITE THE TANNIN MOLECULES.

With that, the Doctor rushes to the kitchen and crams as many teabags as he can into a pot – tannin being a key ingredient in tea …

Soon he is back at Craig's side.

GOOD – HE SEEMS TO BE COMING AROUND.

I'VE … GOT … TO … GO … TO … WORK.

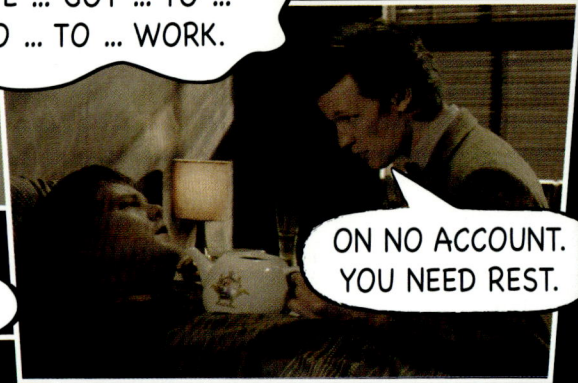

ON NO ACCOUNT. YOU NEED REST.

BUT – BUT – THE PLANNING MEETING. IT'S … VITALLY IMPORTANT.

YOU'RE IMPORTANT, CRAIG. NOW JUST REST AND YOU'LL BE FINE.

07 14

When Craig finally awakens, hours passed in golden silence suddenly give way …

1445

… to sheer **panic**.

WHAT! NO, NO, NO, **NO!**

The time: 14:47.
The place: The Call Centre.
HUFF, HUFF, HUFF.
OH, AFTERNOON, CRAIG.
I'M **SO** SORRY, MICHAEL, I DON'T KNOW WHAT HAPPENED.
WAIT, WHAT'S HE DOING HERE?
PLEASE HOLD, MR LANG.
FEELING BETTER, CRAIG? I HAD SOME TIME TO KILL – NEVER WORKED IN AN OFFICE.
I CAN TELL. WHAT ARE YOU DOING WITH LANG, ONE OF MY BEST CUST– ?
LEAVE OFF THE DOCTOR, CRAIG. HE WAS BRILLIANT IN THE PLANNING MEETING, AND WITH THE CALLS.
HE WENT TO THE PLANNING MEETING?
YES, REPRESENTING YOU. IN FACT, IT WAS YOUR IDEA, CRAIG - YOU MUST BE ILL INDEED. IF YOU'LL JUST RUN BACK HOME, I'LL CONTINUE WITH MY - OUR - WORK.
RUN HOME? YES. THAT GIVES ME A CHANCE ...

... TO SEE WHAT IT IS HE'S REALLY HIDING.

But soon enough he hears the Doctor in the front hall.

Craig decides to use the peephole to find out who the Doctor is speaking to.

WHAT THE — ?

HAVE YOU EVER SEEN ANYONE GO UP THERE ...?

LOTS OF PEOPLE? GOOD, GOOD ...

OH. PEOPLE WHO NEVER COME BACK DOWN. THAT'S NOT SO GOOD.

A moment later.

OH, HELLO.

I CAN'T TAKE THIS ANY MORE. I WANT YOU TO GO! AND YOU CAN HAVE YOUR MONEY BACK, TOO.

WHAT HAVE I DONE?

EVERYBODY LOVES YOU, YOU'RE BETTER AT FOOTBALL THAN ME — AND MY JOB — AND NOW SOPHIE'S ALL, "OH, MONKEYS, MONKEYS!" AND THEN ...

FOR A START, TALKING TO A CAT!

LOTS OF PEOPLE TALK TO CATS.

... **THERE'S THAT!**

LISTEN, ME AND YOU - IT'S JUST NOT GOING TO WORK OUT. THESE HAVE BEEN THE THREE **WEIRDEST** DAYS OF MY LIFE.

THAT? WHY, IT'S ART! YOU KNOW, MODERN ART!

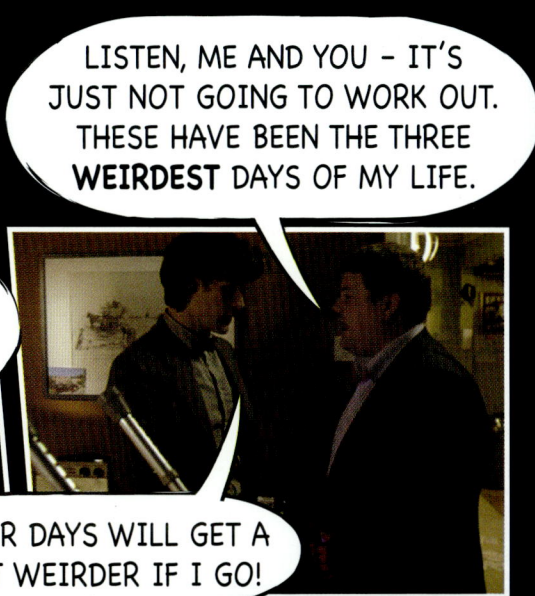

YOUR DAYS WILL GET A LOT WEIRDER IF I GO!

I THOUGHT IT WAS 'GOOD' WEIRD, BUT IT'S NOT. IT'S 'BAD' WEIRD! I TELL YOU, I CAN'T DO THIS ANY MORE!

DON'T YOU SEE? I MUST STAY.

NO, YOU MUSTN'T. YOU MUST LEAVE!

BUT CRAIG, I CAN'T LEAVE THIS PLACE. I'M LIKE YOU - I JUST CAN'T SEE THE POINT OF ANYWHERE ELSE.

I CAN'T GO!

ALL RIGHT, YOU'VE LEFT ME NO CHOICE.

WHAT - WHAT DO YOU MEAN?

JUST GET OUT!

I KNOW I'LL REGRET THIS, BUT ... JUST HOLD STILL ... !

Chapter 5: Showdown!

With an odd lack of anger, the Doctor head butts Craig.

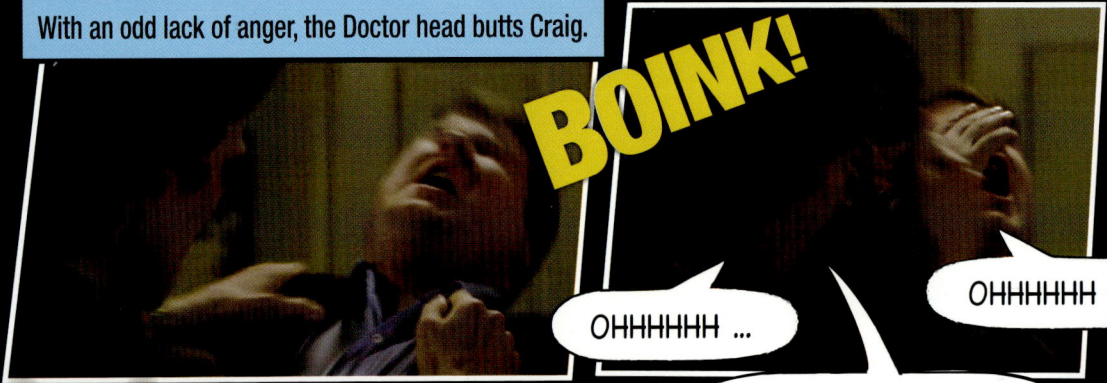

BOINK!

OHHHHHH ...

OHHHHHH ...

ALL RIGHT, THEN. FIRST, GENERAL BACKGROUND ...

In a split second, Craig learns everything important about the Doctor – how he is really a Time Lord and all his past adventures. He even learns that the Doctor's appearance has changed many times over the years.

YOU'RE A ...

YES. SSSHHH!

YES.

FROM ...

SSSHHH. NOT SO LOUD!

YOU'VE GOT A TARDIS!

... NOW ON TO SPECIFIC DETAIL!

BOINK!

DOCTOR - THIS ONE

NO. 79A AICKMAN ROAD

Amy xx ✓

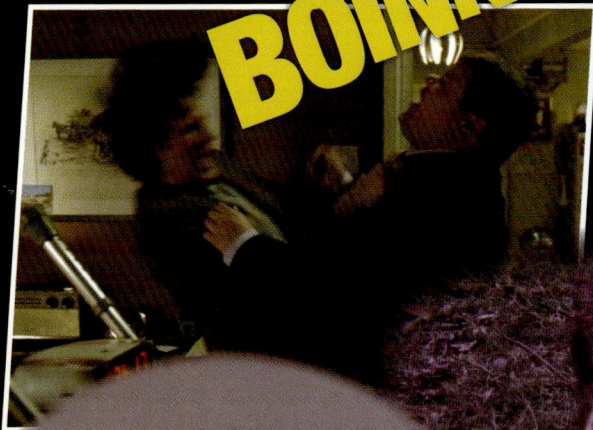

This time Craig learns why the Doctor wanted to be his flatmate – and his suspicions about the upstairs lodger.

YOU SAW MY AD IN THE PAPER SHOP WINDOW!

YES, WITH AMY'S NOTE ABOVE IT. WHICH IS ODD, BECAUSE AMY HASN'T WRITTEN IT YET. TIME TRAVEL, YOU KNOW.

THEN THIS THING IN HERE IS A SCANNER! IT —

BE QUIET! WE CAN'T LET HIM HEAR US!

WE DON'T KNOW WHAT HE MAY TRY NEXT!

SURE, MY NAME'S SOPHIE.

PLEASE CAN YOU HELP ME?

NOW, WHAT'S THE MATTER, MY LOVE?

PLEASE. WILL YOU HELP ME?

AMY!

THAT'S AMY POND! I CAN UNDERSTAND EVERYTHING NOW!

YES, BUT HELP YOU **HOW**?

COME. I'LL SHOW YOU ...

AMY, HAVE YOU GOT THOSE PLANS YET? I HAVE THE FEELING WE'RE RUNNING OUT OF TIME HERE ...

STILL SEARCHING FOR THEM!

AMY, HE'S GOT A TIME ENGINE IN THE FLAT UPSTAIRS. AND HE'S USING INNOCENT PEOPLE TO TRY AND LAUNCH IT.

I'VE WORKED IT OUT WITH PSYCHIC HELP FROM A CAT.

A CAT?

BUT WHENEVER HE DOES ... THEY GET BURNT UP

THAT'S WHY THE STAIN — !

CRAAAAASSSHHH!!!

The TARDIS again shakes violently ...

YOU MEAN PEOPLE ARE DYING UP THERE?

smash!

spark!

SIZZZZLE!

I'M TRYING!

AMY, HOLD ON!

LET'S GO! SOMEONE'S UP THERE RIGHT NOW!
IT MIGHT BE SOPHIE! SHE SAID SHE'D BE COMING OVER...!
HANG ON, SOPHIE!
DOCTOR!
HANG ON, AMY!
DOCTOR, **STOP!!**
ARE YOU UPSTAIRS RIGHT NOW?
JUST GOING IN!
BUT YOU CAN'T BE UPSTAIRS.
OF COURSE I CAN BE UPSTAIRS!
COME ON, LET'S GO IN!
NO! I'VE GOT THE PLANS, YOU CAN'T BE UPSTAIRS! IT'S A ONE-STOREY BUILDING.
THERE IS NO UPSTAIRS!

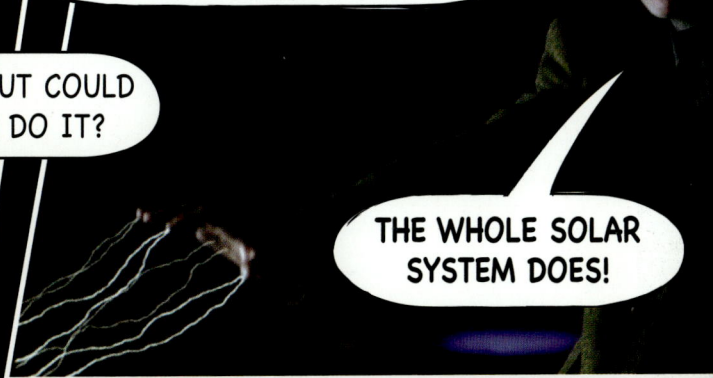

THE CORRECT PILOT HAS BEEN FOUND.
THE KEY IS THAT IT DOESN'T WANT **EVERYONE**. WHY IS THAT? CRAIG, IT DIDN'T WANT YOU ...
I SPOKE TO HIM AND HE SAID THAT I COULDN'T HELP HIM!
NO, THAT'S THE **WORST CHOICE EVER**, I PROMISE YOU. NOW STOP THIS!
DOCTOR, IT'S GETTING WORSE HERE!
AND IT NEVER WANTED ME BEFORE, BUT NOW IT DOES. SO WHAT CHANGED?
OH, NO! GROAN.
THAT MEANS I CAN SHUT DOWN THE ENGINE BECAUSE I DON'T WANT TO LEAVE. I'M MR SOFA MAN, REMEMBER?
I GAVE SOPHIE THE IDEA OF LEAVING! SINCE THIS MACHINE NEEDS TO LEAVE, IT WANTS PEOPLE WHO WANT TO ESCAPE!
YES! SO JUST PUT YOUR HAND ON THE PANEL AND CONCENTRATE ON **WHY YOU WANT TO STAY!**
CRAIG, BE CAREFUL!
I KNOW, SOPHIE. BUT IF THE DOCTOR THINKS IT WILL WORK ...
... THAT'S GOOD ENOUGH FOR ME!
GERONIMO!
SSSSZZZZZZZZZZZZ-
CRAAACKLE!

Now free, the Doctor runs to Craig's side.

CRAIG, WHAT'S KEEPING YOU HERE? THINK ABOUT EVERYTHING THAT MAKES YOU WANT TO STAY!

FOCUS! WHY DON'T YOU WANT TO LEAVE?

IT'S SOPHIE! I DON'T WANT TO LEAVE HER! I CAN'T LEAVE HER!

I LOVE SOPHIE!

When Sophie slams her hand next to Craig's, signalling her desire to stay as well, it seems that the emotion is too much for the alien craft to handle.

I LOVE YOU, TOO, CRAIG, YOU IDIOT!

HONESTLY, SOPHIE, DO YOU MEAN THAT?

OF COURSE I MEAN IT! DO YOU MEAN IT?

I'VE ALWAYS MEANT IT! NOW, WHAT ABOUT THOSE MONKEYS ...?

45

OH, NOT NOW, CRAIG! THE PLANET'S ABOUT TO BURN!

And so ...

FOR GOD'S SAKE, **KISS THE GIRL!**

YES, KISS THE GIRL!!

Everything returns ...

... to normal again.

A BIG YES!

Except ...

... for the hologram, that is.

A BIG NO! WE DIDN'T TURN IT OFF, SO NOW IT'S DOING AN EMERGENCY SHUTDOWN.

HELP ME.

HELP ME!

HELP ME!

THAT MEANS IT'S IMPLODING. EVERYBODY OUT...!

As they rush to escape, the whole house begins to shake.

NOW!

Rrrrruuuuuumble nnnnnnnnn--

But soon they are safely watching from across the street …

… as the true shape of the alien space ship finally **appears** …

… and **disappears**.

REMEMBER THE PERCEPTION FILTER, CRAIG. THERE NEVER **WAS** A TOP FLOOR.

LOOK AT THOSE PEOPLE WALKING BY, DOCTOR. DON'T THEY SEE THAT? THE WHOLE TOP FLOOR HAS VANISHED.

AND WITH THAT, I BELIEVE MISS POND AND I SHOULD BE ON OUR WAY …

And so a few minutes later …
HEY, WAIT UP!
ARE YOU TRYING TO SNEAK OFF?
YES, WELL, I FELT THAT YOU TWO WOULD FINALLY WANT SOME TIME ALONE.
TRUE. BUT I ALSO WANT YOU TO KEEP THESE. THANK YOU.
BECAUSE I MIGHT POP BACK. IS THAT IT?
YES, BUT IF YOU DO, MAKE IT SOON. OTHERWISE WE MIGHT BE IN PARIS.
OR IN THE JUNGLE WITH THE MONKEYS.
WHATEVER YOU TWO DO, I WON'T FORGET YOU. THANK YOU FOR EVERYTHING.
AH, AMY, IT'S SO GOOD TO BE BACK!
AND IT'S GOOD TO HAVE YOU BACK! WHERE TO NOW? ANOTHER EXCITING ADVENTURE IN SOME FAR CORNER OF THE UNIVERSE?
NOT SO FAST! FIRST WE NEED TO GO BACK IN TIME THREE DAYS.
ONLY THREE DAYS? BUT WHY?
BECAUSE YOU STILL NEED TO LEAVE ME THAT NOTE AT THE PAPER SHOP!